Air of Mann

AERIAL VIEWS OF THE ISLE OF MAN

Photography by **Michael Thompson**

Editor **Miles Cowsill**

Text by **Roy McMillan**

Designed by **Tracey Harding**

Published by **Lily Publications Ltd**

Lily Publications
Limited

**PO Box 33 Ramsey
Isle of Man IM99 4LP**

Telephone **01624 898446**

Fax **01624 898449**

ISBN **1 899602 81 X**

Acknowledgements: **Dr Brian Stowel, Phil Harrison and Pat Somner**

FOREWORD

had been talking and thinking about doing an aerial photography book since I saw a display of aerial photography when stranded in Bruxelles airport some time ago. After the success of our first book Spirit of Mann this seemed an interesting and exciting way of showing the Island from a different viewpoint.

The photographs were taken over the first six months of 2001 and were naturally dependent on the weather - as is often the case with the Island's fickle atmospheric conditions. It was so important to have clear bright weather to create shadows, without which the shapes on the ground would have no form. As with all photography, patience is paramount.

The photography in this book would not have been possible without the sympathetic and patient attitude of the pilot, Phil Harrison, to whom I am very grateful. He would take me up in his Cessna C172H flying as low and slow as permitted. I was able to shoot through the open window using a Mamiya 654, with a 105-210 zoom lens, and took the vast majority of the shots on Fuji Provia 400 F film. Practically all the exposures were 1/500 at f11. The zoom lens proved especially useful, since it meant we didn't constantly need to adjust the altitude of the plane.

The basic plan was to cover the whole island with a mixture of towns, villages, and countryside, but I was constantly on the lookout for interesting views, which are only apparent from the air. There are some pictures I like particularly because of the way they relate one part of the Island to another, which would not be possible from the ground. The way Ramsey sits behind Maughold Head (page 48), for example or the view across Fort Island past Derbyhaven and Castletown to Port St. Mary and the Calf (page 139).

In the end, over 500 pictures were whittled down to the ones in the book. Deciding which went in was a joint effort between Miles and myself, but none the easier for that. I hope this book gives pleasure to many and achieves what I set out to do -throw a different light on the familiar and beautiful landscape of the Isle of Man.

Michael Thompson

Corrin's Tower standing at the top of Peel hill. Also known as **Corrin's Folly**, this tower was built in 1806 by Thomas Corrin, who was an uncompromising non-comformist. In order to prove that it was possible to be buried outside consecrated ground, he transferred the remains of his wife and two children to a plot beside the tower. There is still a rumour that he himself, when he died in 1845, was originally buried within church grounds, and then secretly disinterred by friends, to be reburied near his landmark. Rather disappointingly for lovers of intrigue, his burial next to his family was openly reported in contemporary accounts, which referred to the place as the "Dissenter's burial ground".

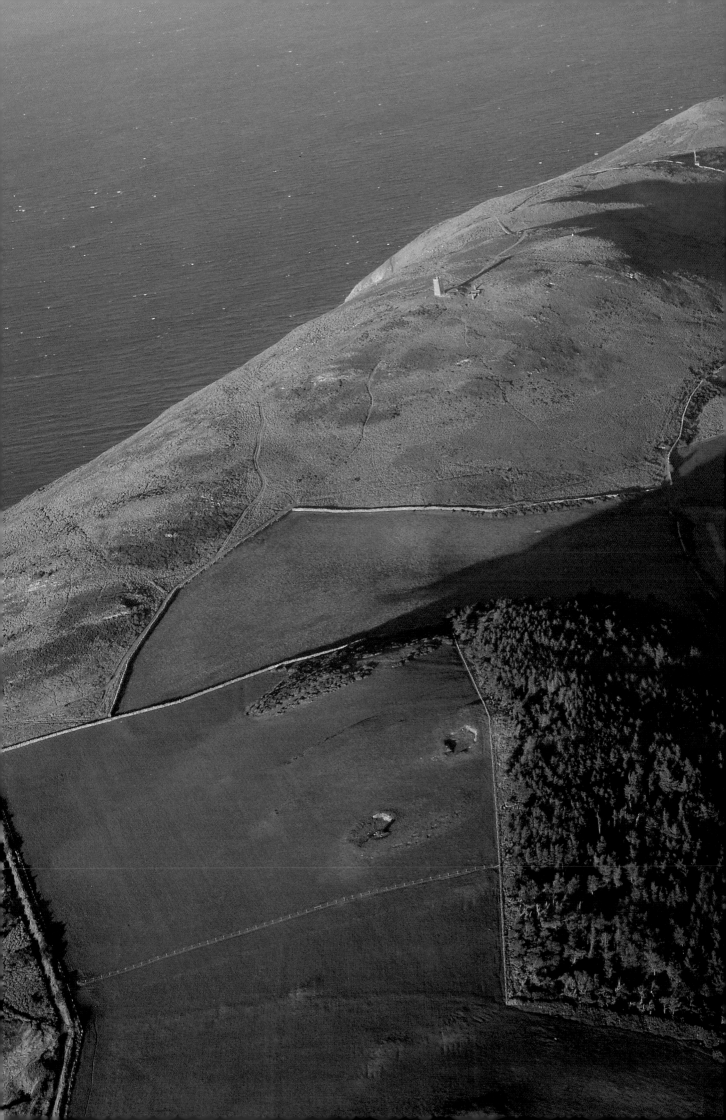

International Alliance Leicester

PO Box 226, 19/21 Prospect Hill, Douglas,
Isle of Man, IM99 1RY.
Telephone: (01624) 663566. Fax: (01624) 663577.
Website: www.alliance-leicester.co.im

CHRYSTALS

ESTATE AGENTS • VALUERS • SURVEYORS

Shane Magee at 31 Victoria Street, Douglas,
Isle of Man, IM1 2SE.
Telephone: (01624) 623778. Fax: (01624) 623284.
E-mail:douglas@chrystals.co.im
www.chrystals.co.im

ISLE OF MAN BANK

PO Box 13, 2 Athol Street, Douglas,
Isle of Man, IM99 1AN.
Telephone: (01624) 637000.

Isle of Man Post Office, Philatelic Bureau,
PO Box 10M, Douglas, Isle of Man, IM99 1PB.
Telephone: (01624) 698430. Fax (01624) 698434.
E-mail: stamps@po.gov.im
Website: www.gov.im/stamps

Department of Tourism and Leisure,
Sea Terminal Buildings, Douglas, Isle of Man, IM1 2RG.
Telephone: (01624) 686801. Website: www.visitIsleofMan.com

LEXICON BOOKSHOP
Est. 1936

63 Strand Street, Douglas, Isle of Man, IM1 2RL.
Telephone: (01624) 673004.
www.LexiconBookshop.co.im

Lloyds TSB

Lloyds TSB Bank (Isle of Man) Limited,
PO Box 111, Peveril Buildings, Peveril Square, Douglas,
Isle of Man, IM99 1JJ. Telephone: (08457) 449900.
www.lloydstsb-offshore.com

Lught-Reill Lectraghys Manninagh
Manx Electricity Authority
PO Box 177, Douglas, Isle of Man, IM99 1PS.
Telephone: (01624) 687687.

manx independent carriers

Distribution Centre, Snugborough Trading Estate, Braddan,
Isle of Man, IM4 4LG. Telephone: (01624) 620185.

IOM Business Park, Cooil Road, Braddan,
Isle of Man, IM99 1HX.
Telephone: (01624) 636616. Fax: (01624) 636616.
www.manx-telecom.com

SINGER & FRIEDLANDER **SF** (ISLE OF MAN) LIMITED

PO Box 197, Samuel Harris House, 5-11 St Georges Street,
Douglas, Isle of Man, IM99 1SN. Telephone: (01624) 699222.
E-mail: info@iom.singer-friedlander.com

Skyefid Limited

2 Water Street, Ramsey, Isle of Man, IM8 1JP.
Telephone: (01624) 811611 Fax: (01624) 816645.
E-mail: mail@skyefid.com

Standard Bank Offshore

Standard Bank House, One Circular Road, Douglas,
Isle of Man, IM1 1SB.
Telephone: (01624) 643643. Fax: (01624) 643800.
Website: www.sboff.com E-mail: sbiom@sboff.com

The coastal stretch between Peel and Ramsey is one of the Island's finest. Although the sea and wind are eroding much of the coastline, and taking it up to the north of the Island, there are still rocky cliff-faces to view, and in particular the **Gob y Deigan caves**. The name translates as either 'Mouth of the Devil' or 'Point of the Daagan' (a kind of fishing-boat) depending on your superstitious tendency. The land above is worked to the very limits of a farmer's skill.

Following pages
Government Offices and the Courts. The Island's legislative and judicial heart in Douglas. Government Offices, Tynwald and the Keys, and the new law courts and registries.

INTRODUCTION

A photograph is supposed, traditionally at least, to capture a moment in time, to be a snapshot of an event or a person. In the very good ones, that captured moment sums something up, holds the essence of the subject. Frequently, however, it is no more than a glimpse, an aide-memoire, and if you're not familiar with the camera it is just a blur with perhaps a bit of thumb in the corner. 'Spirit of Mann', the sister publication to this one, is one book that has shown how something more evanescent can be caught, something that is more than just the thing in the picture. This book takes a different perspective but aims to achieve a very similar effect.

The matter of perspective is crucial. Apart from anything else, it is the reason this book was produced. But there is something elemental about being able to be above the world, both literally and metaphorically. Man has always wanted to fly, to be free of the earth. This may be simply a means of escaping the immediate pressures on the ground – the need to earn, eat and try to be happy – but it is also an attempt to put the environment into perspective. In many ways, the world makes more sense from above. To some extent, there is the novelty value of recognising a place seen from a strange viewpoint. But there are other benefits. It is possible to see how complex systems relate to each other without the usual noise and hubbub of the surroundings. Looking down on a townscape, the road system makes sense, even if finding your way around the one-way system when actually there, is incomprehensible. There is a geometry to the roads as they converge on a town – Andreas, say – which is almost as appealing as the route of a stream. The spread of houses out to the surrounding fields, the way a place sits in its natural environment, the relative scale of neighbouring buildings and developments become clearer.

Douglas is a case in point. The town has changed dramatically in some ways, in others hardly at all. From a plane, the way the commercial centre has spread, with the houses making way for the business headquarters, is a whole social history in one frame. It is so visible in the photograph because it captures it all in a manner that cannot be achieved by the usual means. For those living in the town itself, the shift, while far from imperceptible, has had to have a local impact – everyone notices a car-park being built in their back yard – or be seen in terms of trends – "It were all fields when I were a lad". But to see just how much impact the development has had requires this otherwise unobtainable view.

It is also, of course, a form of reference. Find a landmark in any of the town pictures and work out where your home is, or favourite walk, or building. Once again, it shows more of itself than you can see from the ground. Houses whose frontage you may know well are seen to be shrouded from all sides by trees, except on that small part of it you know. It is also about context. It is possible to see how well or ill something fits with its neighbours. For those interested in the local gossip (skeet), of course, there is also the pleasure of seeing what is in other people's back gardens.

But it is much more than just a chance to see the world as planners imagine it when deciding on the next road scheme or estate, or to have a sly nose around the ginnels. That shift of the lens to the sky reveals the natural world in a different light, too. The way Langness, Derbyhaven and Port St Mary sit at the water's edge, or the flow of the hills down the west coast to the Calf – these are views that can only be found from the air. In the same way that the villages and towns show their hidden designs, so the landscapes become clearer in terms of their relationship to their surroundings. The Sulby reservoir is an example. In one sense, the massive engineering task of building it has been well disguised by the landscaping and planting around it, melting it back into the hillside. From the ground, this is almost impossible to determine, even if you were aware of it in the first place. From the air, this is visible. But the aerial shot also shows how geometric the shape is, how it carves into the land. It also shows how well it fits into its surroundings and illustrates how the streams that meet at that point make it an ideal place for a reservoir.

The book is also a sensual pleasure. The lushness of the valleys and glens, the startling clarity and blueness of the seas, as well as the striking shots of industrial scarring or exposed natural features are breathtaking. This may be because of the distancing that is inevitable in getting above things. The gorse and bracken are romantically rugged if you are not struggling to control it or getting scratched by it, and sharp slopes all the more appealing if you're not trying to climb them.

But perhaps the most remarkable thing about these photographs is how much they manage to show more than just the present. Almost every picture has a hint or an example of what the land was, how it was used and why the Isle of Man used it in that way. There are personal stories buried in each field as well as in every house, and although the intimate may be lacking from this book, it is never impersonal. People stamped themselves on the landscape as much as the land shaped them. The Isle of Man's development from a fishing culture to an industrial one, through tourism and finance, is as discernible as a family likeness through the generations.

X marks the spot where **Alberta Drive** and **Royal Avenue** intersect in **Onchan.**

Following pages
Douglas the capital.

Looking down to the port of **Douglas,** the lifeboat house is at the bottom right. The large white building is the headquarters of a maritime company, built on the site of the former **Fort Anne Hotel** – originally **Sir William Hillary's** home. The Ben My Chree – flagship of the Isle of Man Steam Packet Company – is in dock.

The **Sea Terminal's** striking design (by C. J. Kneen, of Davison and Marsh) mirrors the three legs of Man, although that is only evident when seen from above. Originally, the top floor was a restaurant (The Crow's Nest), but is now home to the Departments of Transport and Tourism and Leisure.

Known colloquially as the "Lemon Squeezer", the Sea Terminal in Douglas was a significant investment in the future when opened in July 1965 by the visiting Princess Margaret. It was seen as representing a progressive and modern outlook on an Island where tourism numbers were down, but the industry itself was still the economic mainstay.

Right
Looking rather like the backbone of a herring, the new pontoons in **Douglas** harbour are ready to receive yachts and boats in a water-retention scheme that is already making the quayside livelier. In the distance, a reminder of the somewhat less leisurely aspects of sailing – the **Tower of Refuge**, built in 1832 both as a warning to ships that the dangerous **Conister Rock** was there, and a place to take shelter if your ship foundered. Inside there was a bell, blankets and food. The tower was the idea of Sir William Hillary, who had founded what became the Royal National Lifeboat Institution eight years previously.

It starts with **Victoria**, becomes a substantial **Prospect** and ends up as **Bucks** ... the last 100 years of Manx history in the name of the road running up the centre of this picture, flanked by the Governmental, legal, ecclesiastical and financial institutions.

Right
For the last three centuries, **Douglas** has been the centre of whatever trade was the Island's staple. Smuggling in the 18th century, trade and tourism in the 19th and early 20th, and now the finance industry. Its architecture has naturally reflected that, and the spread of corporate culture has significantly changed the capital in the last decade. The old terraces, themselves in large part created to rid the capital of filthy slums, have been pushed farther and farther out as the headquarters of businesses located in the finance centre.

Previous pages
The quayside in **Douglas**. The wide-open spaces in the bottom right are demolition scars, soon to be developed. On the left are the light industrial works, with the finance and business heart of the capital on the left.

The latest arrival … the new **Tesco** supermarket in **Douglas** sits beside the bus depot and the Victorian red brick **Railway Terminus** (upper right), which is rather dwarfed by the newcomer.

Demolition and renewal – the **Royal Bank of Scotland International** building with its roof garden is a major landmark on the promenade in Douglas. Its modern Deco feel is reminiscent of the prow of an ocean liner, but it is still an unfinished building, with much work to do around it to complete the plans of the designers. Behind it is the alternative method of modernising – the original shell of the **Grand Hotel** now houses finance and insurance companies.

Left
The picture shows the increasing demand for car parking and the spread of the business centre pushing housing further out of the centre of town.

Previous pages
Douglas from the **quay** in the bottom left up to the **new courthouse** and **registry offices** in the upper right, and the hospital top centre. The two churches in the middle are **St George's**, the oldest church in Douglas (1781), and **St Mary of the Isle**, a Roman Catholic church built in 1859.

The public and private sectors in close company. The gold-domed top of the **Standard Bank** building is opposite the **Law Courts**. The large building in the bottom right is home to three **Government** departments – although one is about to relocate to the large building on the far left.

Villa Marina and Gaiety Theatre – The glass Toblerone of the Sefton Hotel's new atrium is the principal modern addition in this picture of Harris Promenade in Douglas at low tide. The Villa Marina and its gardens dominate, although the concrete additions to the original serve to almost entirely obscure it. But some alterations are more difficult to see – underneath the newly laid Promenade walkway is the IRIS scheme for the capital's sewage.

St Ninian's High School and Bray Hill – The semi-circles of houses on Inner Circle, High View Road and Port-e-Chee Avenue, with their detached be-gardened residences facing the terraces of Lancaster, Hildesley and Malvern Roads, showing how housing in the capital has changed.

Right
St Ninian's and Environs – St Ninian's Church, another gift of Henry Bloom Noble (in 1888), commands magnificent views over Douglas. Just across the road is St Ninian's High School.

The sweep of **Alexander Drive** in **Douglas**.

Woodbourne Square with Park – Woodbourne Square is one of several similar schemes in Douglas, involving terraced town-houses overlooking a private area of grass or parkland.

Government House, on the outskirts of Onchan, is not where the government is housed. It is the official residence of the Lieutenant Governor, the representative of the British Crown. The name of the house might seem inappropriate or at the least a little confusing - it has never housed government at all. It was originally owned by the Heywood family, and known as Bemahague. Governor Loch leased it in 1865 as his official residence at a time when it was becoming clear the capital would have to be Douglas rather than Castletown. The Manx government bought it in 1903, and that's why it's called Government House. It may also serve as a means of reminding the Lieutenant Governor that he is a guest in someone else's house.

Coutt's Bank in **Onchan**. A substantial building, the three terraced houses beside it look as if they could fit in its portico

The spine of well-proportioned houses that is **Royal Avenue West** snakes up from the bottom left, with **Onchan Pleasure Park** behind it. Beyond, the expanding town of **Onchan** itself.

Royal Avenue with **St Peter's Church** in **Onchan**. The church stands on ground that has been sanctified for over a thousand years.
Vikings worshipped here, and the village takes its name from St Connaghyn. The church on the land before St Peter's was built in
1833 was called Kirk Conchan, is another spelling of the saint's name. This in turn became Kirk Onchan. In 1781, a William Bligh,

later to become famous (or notorious depending on which revision of the story you believe) as captain of H.M.S. Bounty, was married here to Elizabeth Beetham. Neither was Manx, but the Island's connection with the Bounty was cemented when Fletcher Christian joined the crew, and the Bounty once landed in Douglas

Recent estimates suggest the Isle of Man's growing and changing population will require about 3,500 houses in the next decade. That is effectively a house a day for the next ten years. About 3 weeks' worth is seen here under construction near **Howstrake** in **Onchan**.

Far left
Part of the Dandara Group's **Governor's Hill** development on the border between **Onchan** and **Douglas**, showing the lakes. While these are an attractive scenic feature, and have proved very popular with ducks, they are also a crucial part of the drainage system. If the water from the houses were allowed to flow directly into the streams that lead down through **Summerhill Glen**, they would overwhelm it. A valve situated in the upper of the four lakes (known as "balancing ponds") allows them to collect the water, and release it at a manageable rate.

Previous pages
King Edward Bay Apartments and continuing development on **Onchan Head**, with the stadium and park in the upper right. **Summerland** and the **Aquadrome** are at the end of **Douglas** promenade.

If there were pools in the back yards, it could be the States … The final phase of **Birchill** in **Onchan**, completed in the spring of 2000.

Signpost Corner. The **TT course** arrives at the bottom left, and screams round the roundabout to the right. If you were to go straight ahead towards the top of the picture, you would be in **Heywood Park**, built in 1992.

The electric railway takes a slightly more scenic route. The railway was extended to Laxey in 1894 having been built as far as **Groudle** the previous year.

Lead, copper and **silver** were mined in this region, and it was the mining industry that took **Laxey** from a group of fishermen on the shores of the river near the sea to a village crowding around the new railways and extraction industries up the hill. The hills, now shaded with forest and lush plantation, were comprehensively despoiled by the work – the diggings from the mines were stored in heaps 50ft higher than the cottages at their feet. These hills were the homes of at least four different mines with many different shafts. Other businesses grew in such a fecund atmosphere – carpenters, blacksmiths and all the associated trades of heavy industry, as well as other trades such as papermaking and woollen mills.

The Isle of Man's scenery and countryside, allied to its extraordinary history, are seen as major selling points to the tourist industry. Less well-known is its industrial past, yet the **Lady Isabella** – the **Laxey Wheel** – is one of the most photographed and celebrated monuments to mining in the British Isles – and with some reason. Capable of pumping 250 gallons of water a minute, the wheel is believed to be the biggest of its type in the world, and the production from its mines of zinc blend (in 1854-55 at any rate) was greater than the combined output of the rest of the British Isles. However, the casting of the Three Legs (said to be the biggest of its kind, as you would expect of such a monumental undertaking) presents the legs running in what is generally accepted to be the wrong way. That is, the legs are running anti-clockwise.

Previous pages
The large, square building is a **pipe factory**, making briar and Meerschaum. As with so many things in **Laxey**, its existence is because of the extraction industries. It was originally used by the mining companies as a warehouse

Laxey harbour. At the height of the industrial work in the area, heavy equipment would be sailed around the coast, dropped onto the seabed at high tide and then retrieved and dragged up to the mines once the tide had fallen

An outcrop of the Manx Slate on the east coast. This rock is the predominant feature of the Island's geology.

The sea at **Port Cornaa**. Even without the temptation of the clear blue sea as it is pictured here, this north-eastern part of the Island has been a habitation for four thousand years. Not far away is **Cashtal yn Ard**, the burial chamber dating back to 2000 BC. More recent attempts to use the fresh running water for industrial rather than domestic purposes were less successful. The Bellite Company wanted to make explosives, but local opposition prevented it.

The Dhoon. The area is now owned by **Manx National Heritage**, and there was once substantial quarrying (principally for granite) at the head of the slopes. This area is also known for its wild goats, some 400 of which roam the forests and fields. It is not an easy glen to get to, being the steepest on the Island, but worth the effort. Its inaccessibility is laconically referred to in the name which may mean 'deep'.

Beyond the Headland, **Ramsey** and the **northern plain**.

Maughold Head is a hamlet on the north east of the Island, and sits on slate cliffs 70 feet above the sea. The rocks are rich in iron, copper, lime and quartz. Its name came from that of an Irish chiefton ruffian called **Maccuil** who mugged **St Patrick**, but was converted by him. As a penance, however, he was set adrift in a coracle wearing leg-irons (or with his hands tied. Neither would have been comfortable) and without food or water. He drifted onto the headland, where he met two Christians called **Conindrus** and **Rumilus**, whereupon he sank to his knees and thanked God for his deliverance. At the point where he knelt, a spring gushed forth, and there are other tales of an ever-flowing spring told on crosses in the churchyard.

The rocky faces of the cliffs are a breeding ground for several rare species of bird, such as cormorants, or at least rare in terms of their location. Swifts and house martins are regular nesters here, despite being better known for living in, on and around buildings. Perching on the headland as if moulded to it is the lighthouse. It was built in 1914, with the engine houses and keepers' lodges on the head itself while the lighthouse is some 170 feet below it, reached by 129 steps. The views of the cliff-faces make it all worth the effort, though, beyond the headland **Ramsey** and the **northern plain**.

The little headland of **Gob ny Rona**. The name translates as **Point of the Seals**, but the area was once mined for iron and there are still remains of a battery on the headland.

Maughold village churchyard. It has a magnificent collection of Celtic crosses, but some visit the cemetery with an interest in a more recent grave. This is where the author **Hall Caine** is buried. Not technically Manx, there was Island blood on his father's side, and he became for some time the world's most famous Manxman. Although his stock is now considerably reduced in the public mind, until his death in 1931, he was one of the most celebrated novelists of his time, more popular than Dickens, with crowds on the quayside in America to receive the latest instalments of his work

The **Ballure plantation** and reservoir. One of the smaller reservoirs on the Island, it was opened in 1858 by the **Ramsey and Northern Water Board**, and is one of three serving the north of the Island. As with all the Island's reservoirs, it is stocked with fish (especially trout) and the fishing season is another one of the Island's temptations to visitors.

The town arms of **Ramsey Harbour** reach out into the sea, looking a little like a pair of forceps. The **South Pier** is over 200 years old, although only extended to its current 570 feet in 1876. The **North Pier** took 26 years to complete between 1842 and 1868.

Ramsey Bay is the clay-bottomed, flat, shallow, sandy stretch of coast from **Maughold** to the **Point of Ayre**. It runs in a gentle sweep for over ten miles, and presents a coastline that is well-protected from the westerlies, and is a favoured point for ships looking for shelter in a storm – such as the one carrying Queen Victoria and Prince Albert in 1847 which docked unexpectedly. Prince Albert wanted to get some fresh air (and away from a ship filled with seasick people) and asked the first person he met – the barber - to take him for a walk up Lhergy Frissell hill. Albert's walk there was commemorated by the erection of a tower, apparently because, in a manner not unlike the current Duke of Edinburgh, he made a point of telling the barber that there should be a tower there anyway. While Albert was enjoying the view, word of his arrival spread around the Island, and the Governor, who lived in Castletown, set about heading northward as fast as his carriage would take him. Unfortunately, he could only manage to reach Ramsey as the royal boat passed out of sight. It is said the Bishop managed an audience with Queen Victoria, who had stayed on board.

Pictures of Ramsey from the past suggest it looks in many ways much as it did a hundred years ago, with several of the buildings surviving perfectly, from warehouses to chandlers. To some this is precisely why any development needs to be carried out with the utmost care for the atmosphere of the town; to others it demonstrates a lack of entrepreneurial daring.

The **Mooragh Park** and associated amenities was originally wasteland, turned to productive use to take advantage of the visitors. Because of the low-lying and frequently rather damp nature of much of the area ('mooragh' means 'void place cast up by the sea', although a less nihilistic translation might be 'shingle beach'), a new promenade and sea wall were needed to keep people dry enough to enjoy the facilities. It opened a year after the **Queen's Pier**, and is still popular.

The Sulby winds into Ramsey, widening as it surrounds what was once the shipbuilders' yards. Shipbuilding was successful in Ramsey between 1839 and the 1960s, in an area where there is still a 'Shipyard Road'. Gibson's of Newcastle took over the firm J. Taggart and Co and gradually built the business up until it was employing 250 men and making ships of up to 2,000 tons. The most famous was the **Euterpe** – renamed the **Star of India**. The demand for bigger and bigger ships, however, saw the industry die.

Previous pages
The **Mooragh Park**, Ramsey harbour and the **Queen's Pier**. The latter was part of the revolution in transport and tourism that made the Island successful in the late 19th century. There was always a danger that Ramsey would be isolated from the tourist trade without adequate travel provision. Trains were one – and with the construction of the Queen's Pier in 1886, people could arrive by sea at whatever state of the tide. It was designed by Sir John Coode, reached out 2,248 feet, and had a little tramway to transport you to and from the shore. However, it fell into desuetude and its future is uncertain.

The **swing bridge** crosses the harbour. The bridge serves to link the quayside with the **Mooragh Park** area to the north, and was built in 1892. At the time, the engineering firm responsible – Cleveland Bride of Darlington – thought pink and maroon was a pleasing colour combination. Its recent restoration has, thankfully, reverted to a more sober scheme.

Left
Ramsey Harbour has changed as the river mouth has moved. The Sulby at one point made the town effectively an island, but it has been tamed somewhat now. The buildings around the quay and harbour are remarkable remnants of the great days of the sea – chandlers, warehouses, customs posts and the like. Modern developments include the Shoprite supermarket and the Wessex garage (bottom centre and right).

Previous pages
Safe haven. **The Sulby** meets the sea under the **swing bridge**.

Ramsey Cottage Hospital. Henry Bloom Noble didn't reserve his philanthropy for Douglas. The cottage hospital was founded in 1907 with funds from the great benefactor.

The most northerly village on the Island, **Bride**.

The **northern plain**, looking back from the **Point of Ayre**. These flatlands were caused by glacial drift, and it is suggested that without the deposits left after the last ice age the northern plain would still be under water, with the background hills the preglacial shoreline. The whole area is of outstanding importance for wildlife, and is home to some of the rarest plants on the Island. In the 1900s, after a discovery of brine some way under the surface, there was a plan to turn Ramsey into a spa town. Bore-holes 800 metres deep were sunk, and pipes laid to take the health-giving fluid to the town. But a combination of environmental opposition and ill-considered positioning of the pipes brought an end to the scheme.

The **northern tip of the Island** with **Maughold** behind. The area is used as the principal landfill site for the Island. Happily, the sites have proved popular with birdlife, and once capacity is reached in the landfills, the area will be comprehensively landscaped, and native fauna reintroduced.

The **lighthouse** at the **Point of Ayre**. This is another one by **Robert Stevenson**, constructed in 1862, but work didn't go as smoothly as had been hoped; Stevenson personally sacked the Inspector of Works when he was inspecting the tower. The main lighthouse is now a quarter of a mile from the coast it was originally intended to protect. This is because of a variation on the theme of land reclamation. The tides and winds that are doing so much damage to the coast on the north west of the Island, and moving material from the east, are extending the northern tip. So much so that a second, smaller lighthouse had to be added just 30 years later.

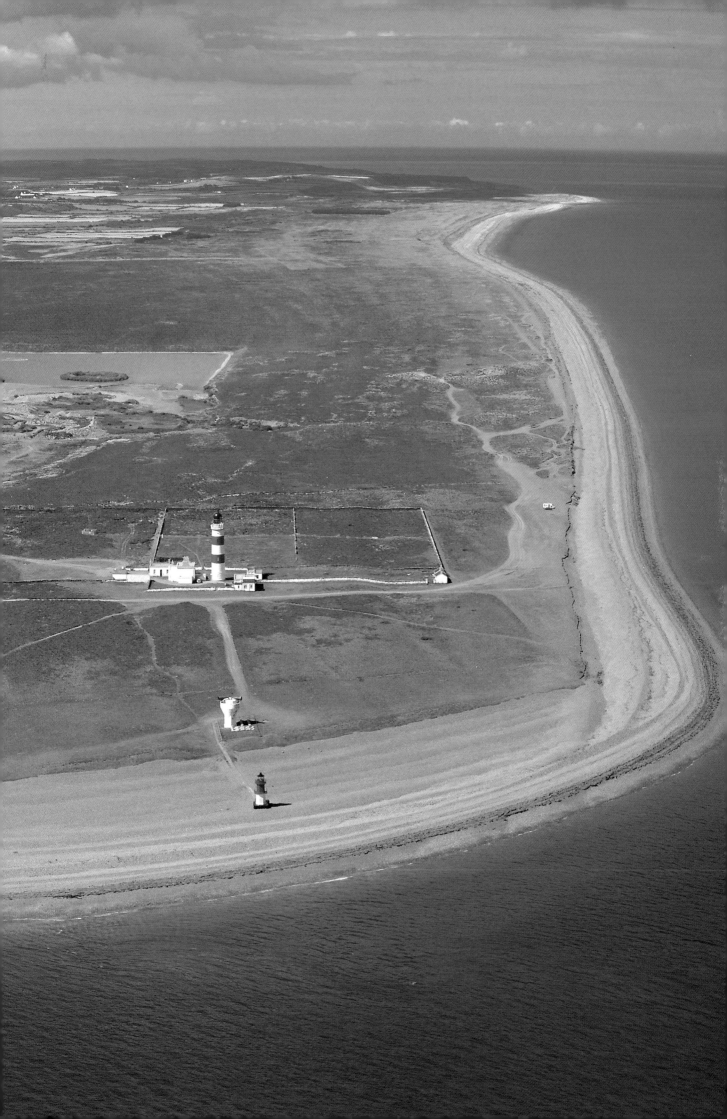

The Lhen Trench meets the Irish Sea. The name possibly means **'The Great Ditch'**, which seems rather less respectful and industrial than the stolid 'trench'. This is perhaps unsurprising. The trench was created – it is thought that it was roughly on the lines of an existing stream – in the 17th century, but was plagued by the need for repairs. As a result, farmers were always being asked to look after their sluices and clean them out. It did make a difference to the landscape, though. The whole of the Island's northern plain was awash, and the Lhen Trench helped to turn it into one of the most fertile regions of the Isle of Man.

The Ayres is a distinctive and divisive region. Some are awed by the sweep of uninhabited coast with its rare plants, heathland dominated by lichen, wildlife found nowhere else on the Island and over four miles of beach with only one building on it – the visitors centre. Others feel the space is too bleak. But the drama of the ridged shingle coastline is undeniable.

Andreas sits in lush agricultural land. The school was originally established in 1838, with the present one built in 1903. The village was until recently the **home of the Island's Archdeacon**, a residency taken up not just because of the quality of the scenery but also because the tithes were more rewarding. Although there has clearly been development here, the area is still used by those with a love of the air. The flat landscape made it ideal for airfields and it was an important base for the RAF during the war. It is still the home of the gliding club.

Originally a 13th century church, **St Patrick's** on the **Jurby** coast was rebuilt in the early 19th century, but used some of the older materials. It now serves as a landmark visible for miles both on land and out at sea. However, its future is a deal less clear, with subsidence causing major structural problems.

At some point, you just have to say enough is enough. An abandoned farmhouse on the rapidly receding coastline just north of **Kirk Michael**. The threat of imminent collapse doesn't stop the farmer from ploughing right up to the edge

Cronk Sumark, in **Sulby**. The hill has at its summit evidence of **Viking** and **Celtic** occupation, and there was probably smelting of some sort done here, since the stones have vitrified. It was also the site of substantial quarrying. Although commonly translated as Primrose Hill ('**sumark**' is thought to be a corruption of the Irish word '**seamrog**', which eventually became anglicised as 'shamrock'. the name may actually mean **Refuge Hill**, since the site was almost certainly fortified. There are many hill-based forts around the Island, and some were in use as late as the early 19th century. The lush fields around the base are nowadays the scene of the **Royal Manx Agricultural Show**.

Ballacuberagh at the entrance to **Sulby Glen**.

Almost flattened here by the angle, the kink in the **TT course** that is the treacherous (but spectacular) **Ballaugh Bridge**

From **Kirk Michael** to **Peel**; the west coast

The **TT course** sweeps through **Kirk Michael** (from top right) past the school, the bank (the square building in its own plot) and then on through the village past the church, burial-place of Bishop Wilson and four other Bishops. The area was considered important in the past because Tynwald is said to have met nearby at Cronk Urleigh, also known as Cronk Urley and Reneurling. Just in case that isn't confusing enough, it may not have been there after all – it could have been Rhencullen.

… but there is more to the town than just the TT course (from bottom right). Development continues on the left towards the coastline.

A view across **Snaefell** looking east over **North Barrule**. The name Barrule could derive from the Old Norse and mean 'ward's mountain'. It was once a matter of some importance to keep a watch over the seas to spy any potential invaders. North Barrule was also the site of one of the Island's greatest tragedies. 31 American airmen died when their plane crashed on April 23rd 1945, just two weeks before the end of the war. There is now a permanent memorial to them at the site.

Left
Sulby Reservoir. Built in 1983 at a cost of £12 million, this massive reservoir holds 1,000 million gallons and was opened by Princess Alexandra.

Previous pages
The coast between **Glen Mooar** and **Peel** on the west of the Island shows how streams and the sea have together moulded the dramatic landscape, and from this angle the land looks like the feet of some huge green monster about to test the water.

The **Sulby Reservoir** has built into it a small hydro-electric plant. It was also intended to house within its workings the nuclear bomb-proof bunker to which politicians would retreat in the event of a war. However, the plan was considered impractical (apart from any other considerations) because it would have taken too long to get the great and the good to the remote location!

Looking over **St John's** and **Greeba** to the distant **Snaefell**.

Peel tumbles towards the sea. It grew as a fishing port, and a significant one for the Island. Its growth in more recent times has not damaged the unique character of the fishing village it once was, at least in the central part of the town, where narrow streets wind down to the quay. The substantial hole dug into the promenade (bottom, centre left) is the IRIS project.

Left
The Island's cathedral, **St German's** in **Peel**. The old church of St German on St Patrick's Isle was the cathedral of the diocese of Sodor and Man, but it had been falling into dilapidation for centuries (one of the 17th century's Bishops, Sam Rutter, invited the reader of his epitaph to "laugh at the Bishop's Palace"). In 1870, Bishop Hill made an attempt to restore it but there was no public support for the idea and the money went instead to St Peter's the Market Square. This was hardly better, and was eventually condemned as insanitary. However, Bishop Hill was an extraordinary fund-raiser, and he managed to find £6,000 to be put towards a new church. This was built in 1884, was met with joy and great celebrations at the time and is the one pictured. But it was a long an uncomfortable road before it became the cathedral. Financial and ecclesiastical problems prevented it, despite petitions, and subsidence in 1906 meant the spire had to be removed. Bishopscourt was a temporary cathedral until 1980, when after nearly a century, St German's was consecrated as the new one. Rather sadly, Bishop Hill himself never wanted it to be the cathedral. His life's ambition was to see the old one on St Patrick's Isle restored. If that were not possible, he felt it should go to one of the bigger churches in Douglas (St Thomas' was his preferred choice), and the one built with money he had raised he felt was too big and too expensive.

Previous pages
Tynwald Hill and **St John's**, the centre of the Island's historic and unique Parliament.

The **House of Manannan** in **Peel**. For some, the fortunes of Peel were transformed by the building of this social history museum. Peel had been a successful fishing port and a popular spot with tourists. But it had missed out on the financial services, and there was a growing worry that too few people were coming out west to visit. Then Manx National Heritage built their museum. It cost £6 million and was named Museum of the Year when it opened in 1997. It sits where once the railway station did – itself a striking Deco design by Armitage Rigby - and the new structure has echoes of that earlier one. It was formally opened on Tynwald Day by the then President of Ireland, Mary Robinson.

The large building at the top right is the Shoprite supermarket on the outskirts of **Peel**. As with all the Island's towns, Peel has spread from its initial harbourside presence to the fields that lay behind the original town.

St Patrick's Isle and **Peel Bay**. The only natural bay on the west coast is defended by the castle that surrounds the old cathedral. It was the building of defences for the area that gave the town its name, deriving from the piles used to create the foundations, or the old English 'peele', fortification. The town's name in Manx **(Purt ny h-Inshey)** means **'Port of the Island'**, but the island it is referring to is not the Isle of Man but St Patrick's Isle. That is how important this small rock was. It is sometimes difficult to detach such a well-known attraction place from its present status and recall its real purpose and significance. This little island off the west coast was probably the home of the Isle of Man's kings until the 13th century. The castle was built to protect the cathedral of St German, but it needed permission from the Pope in 1392. The following two hundred years saw more and more fortification on the site as the threat of attack from any number of directions grew. St Patrick's Isle is some 7 acres in all, but has history, myth and legend seeping from the very earth, rock and red sandstone walls around it. Wordsworth and Scott are just two great writers who have been inspired by the site and its history.

Peel Hill dwarfs **St Patrick's Isle**, in this view looking north up the west coast.

Glen Maye is one of the 17 national glens around the Island. It is as famous for its waterfall as its walks, and almost as well known for its pub. In the 18th century, there were trial mines carried out in the area, but there was insufficient value in what was found.

Following pages
Looking south, down the west coast, to the **Calf of Man**

Bradda Head in **Port Erin** has at its peak another of the Island's landmark towers. This is **Milner's Tower**, built in 1871 by the public in recognition of the work done by William Milner for the town's poor and its fishermen. William Milner was born in Liverpool and was a successful safe-maker. As a result, the tower is designed to resemble a key standing upright. The citizens of Port Erin clearly felt strongly about William Milner. His tower was erected during his lifetime, and St Catherine's Church was built under the directions of his will.

Port Erin Bay, with **Bradda Head** and **Milner's Tower**, looking across to **Port St Mary**. Port Erin probably takes its name from the fact it is the Island's closest port to Ireland.

Previous pages
Port Erin lurks behind the crags of **Bradda Head** and the southern tip of the Island tapers towards the **Calf**.

Port Erin from what is called variously the Castle Rock, the Castle or the Castle Rocks. The shape of the bay made it a natural refuge, and there were several attempts to develop it as such, notably a failed attempt to build a breakwater during the 1880s. Repeated storm damage meant the effort had to be abandoned, but it nearly cost the Island dear. The British Government had donated £58,000, but then stated that this was in fact a loan, repayable with interest. Governor Loch, who had instigated the breakwater (among several other worthwhile and much more successful schemes) had to persuade the British that a repayment of £20,000 would be sufficient. The **Raglan Pier**, where in calm weather there are sailings to the Calf, was opened in 1916.

Copper was mined from a 100-metre deep shaft at **Bradda Head**, and the rocks show the veining of the copper as well as that of quartz. This was once described as "the noblest surface exhibition of a mineral vein to be seen in Europe" by Sir W. W. Smythe.

Previous pages
The massive bulwark of **Bradda Head**, topped with **Milner's Tower**, at the entrance to **Port Erin Bay**.

There is always the problem of what to do with the physical remains of an industry. Hotels into business premises - yes; cafés into private homes – yes, as in the turreted building with the bay window. But what can you do with an old swimming pool? Everyone wants to see something done – but what?

The winding footpaths and the bunkers of the golf course show what brings many people to **Port Erin**, although those little bays, the azure (if rippled) sea and the sandy beaches show it doesn't have to be man-made to be popular. Behind the Victorian sea front, the growing popularity of the south of the Island can be seen in the spread of developments.

The promenade and beach at **Port Erin**, with the inevitable development being carried out. It may appear unattractive, while under construction, but the building of new hotels and apartment blocks is a symbol of the Island's increasing prosperity, and of the higher standards being demanded by the visitors.

Previous pages
Port Erin has grown from a small fishing village – the houses on the beach-front are the remains of that – to a town with an internationally renowned **Marine Laboratory** and an equally respected international arts festival. The laboratory was founded by Sir William Herdman in 1892, and is now a part of the **University of Liverpool**. The arts festival was founded by John Bethell, and attracts major performers from all over the world. Tourism was brought by the railways, but the war brought them, too – in the shape of female and child internees, who were billeted with the locals who owned the hotels built on the upper level of the promenade.

Following pages
Cregneash Village Folk Museum is one of the prides of the **Manx Museum and National Trust**. It had been a crofting community for centuries, and one where Manx Gaelic was still spoken, but it was clear that preserving any sense of the community could not be done in a museum. Thanks to the influences of a Scandinavian academic, Professor Carl Marstrander, the foresight of the Museum's William Cubbon, and the generosity of Harry Kelly's family – who donated his cottage in 1938 – Cregneash became the first publicly-owned, open-air folk museum in the British Isles.

The three lighthouses on the **Calf of Man** represent a tour through the history of lighthouses. It has been suggested there was a beacon on the Calf in medieval times, and there is evidence of a lighthouse proper dating back almost three hundred years. In 1818, the twin light system designed by **Robert Stevenson** became operational. Stevenson was something of a shining light himself, responsible for 23 lighthouses around Scotland, including the Bell Rock off Arbroath. By the late 1860s, however, his work on the Calf was wearing badly. A new lighthouse was built on **Chicken Rock** and began its operational life in 1875.

The **Chicken Rock lighthouse** is solid granite for the first 32 feet, and rises over 120 feet above the sea. A fire in 1960 meant it became automatic, and as a result unoccupied (previously, the lighthouse keeper had lived in the upper sections, and his family in houses in Port St Mary). After 93 years safeguarding the traffic through the treacherous waters around the Calf, the Chicken Rock lighthouse was superseded by the current one, built between the two lights originally designed by Stevenson. This new light has the power of over two million candles, and was officially turned on by the then Lieutenant Governor, Sir Peter Stallard, in July 1968.

Previous pages
The southern tip of the Isle of Man, **The Sound**, with **Thousla Rock** and **Kitterland**, and the **Calf of Man**. It looks calm enough, but the currents and tides between the land masses can be absolutely treacherous. Thousla may mean 'fire rock', which could (although this is deep into speculation) imply a beacon has been there for some time. Kitterland takes its name from a Norse warrior who is said to have foundered there.

The little rock called the **Burroo**, is on the south east of the **Calf**. Despite its remoteness, most of the Calf was farmed, and there are even remains of some defences called Busaell's Grave, on the top of Burroo. It is possible to land at the little bay on the right, and the sea around the Calf is a magnificent place to dive, with clear waters and a superb collection of flora and fauna to see. However, all those who dive here are warned of the dangerous currents and sudden changes in the sea's moods.

Coming in to land at **South Harbour**.

Looking back to the Isle of Man past the **Chicken Rock** and the **Calf**. The Chicken Rock is thought to get its name from the number of stormy petrels that use it. These petrels are known to sailors, apparently, as 'Mother Carey's Chickens'.

Across **Perwick Bay** to **Bradda Head.**

Port St Mary harbour.

Previous pages
From **Kallow Point**, with **Perwick Bay** on the left, across **Port St Mary** to **Port Erin**.

The inner and outer harbours of **Port St Mary**, with **Kallow Point** in the background.

An almost startlingly clear, blue sea at **Chapel Bay** in **Port St Mary**, seen from above **Gansey Point**. The earthworks in the bottom right are – again - for the IRIS scheme.

Left
The smooth, sandy sweep of **Chapel Bay**, and, naturally, the IRIS works.

Chapel Bay from above **Bay ny Carrickey**, looking across to the village of **Port St Mary** itself, the golf course and **Perwick Bay.**

The inner harbour of **Port St Mary**. Despite the growing popularity of the village as a place to live and visit, it has managed to maintain its sense of being a fishing village — even if the boats in the harbour are more likely to be yachts than Nickeys.

Port St Mary's breakwaters allow the port to be accessible whatever the tide. This has led to calls for the Island's first marina to be developed here. The principal protection against the waves is the Alfred Pier, 1,200 feet long and now 120 years old. It was named after Prince Alfred, the Duke of Edinburgh.

Colby was a centre of Methodism in the Island, and in the 19th century there were two chapels (one a Wesleyan, one a Primitive) facing each other across the main road and apparently in some rivalry. The Wesleyan won out in the end – the Primitive closed in 1950.

Impossibly romantic ... a **steam train** from the last century but one pulls the carriages along a stretch of unspoilt countryside between **Douglas** and **Port Erin**.

Following pages
A view across the archaeological site of **Rushen Abbey** to **Ballasalla**. Rushen Abbey is probably the most important ecclesiastical site on the Island, but it has had a fairly hard time of it. Established in 1134, it became the home of a Cistercian order and over the next century and a half grew in power until it had mining rights and over 2,000 acres of land around the Island. Then in the early 14th century it was looted, in 1541 dissolved (the last of the monasteries in the British Isles to suffer the fate) and sold, and left to decay. In the 17th century, there was a plan to establish a school there, but the project never came to anything; in the mid-19th century, the Government intended to turn it into a mental institution, but never realised the plan. It was the site of a nightclub built over the graves of Norse kings while it was privately owned until 1998 when the site was purchased by government. It is now in the hands of Manx National Heritage. The name Ballasalla is another one of the Manx names whose origin depends upon your view of the area. To some, it means Willow Farm; for others, Filthy Farm; and to still others, a saintly farmstead. There is a certain rivalry between the north and south of the Island, and those in the south tend to think Ballasalla actually comes from Balla Saint Lua, or St Lua's farm, and attribute the less appealing derivation to the area in Jurby with the same name.

Ballabeg. The longest established parish fair in the Island, Laa Columb Killey (or "The day of St Columba's Church"), has its origins in the Ballabeg Fair, and is still held here.

St Mark's. The village sits surrounded here by fields but the church and a school were originally created in 1772 for those in the nearby hilly regions.

Previous pages

Across **Castletown**, past **Derbyhaven** and **King William's College** to the runways of **Ronaldsway**.

If the design of King William's College is a little familiar, that shouldn't be too much of a surprise. The architects were Edward and John Welch, who were responsible for the Tower of Refuge and several churches around the Island. The school was opened in 1833, and uses the name of England's king at the time. His name was all he gave, however. A fire just eleven years later almost destroyed the interior, and did destroy a number of irreplaceable books and manuscripts. Additions and extensions appeared regularly throughout its history, but it has remained a successful independent school, until now very much on the lines of a typical English public school. It has recently decided to offer the International Baccalaureate rather than A levels.

Castle Rushen stands proud, surrounded by its 25ft high walls and dominates in both substance and style the town around it. The building just above right is the police station, designed in 1901 by the architect **Mackay Hugh Baillie Scott**. The look of the station was to match the castle, and its stone walls and baronial manner do make it look like a lodge of sorts. Its conical turret and scale however have led to it being called the glue pot, or the 'Toytown' police station.

Malew Street leads past the bowling green and the tennis courts to the town square, and – of course – the castle itself

Looking from **Derbyhaven** to **Castletown**. Development seems to have been controlled and contained in Castletown, although there is pressure for more housing as it becomes more and more popular both for businesses and residents.

Two of the great places of power in the Island stand on either side of the footbridge across the **Silverburn** in **Castletown**. **Castle Rushen**, dominating the town, and Lorne House, almost hidden from it behind its screen of trees. The former was the seat of the ancient Kings and Lords of Mann; the latter the home of the Governors of Mann between 1834 and 1860.

The blue-grey limestone around **Castletown** colours almost all the older buildings, especially **Castle Rushen** itself. The name Rushen is thought to come from the Irish and Gaelic word 'ros', meaning a wood or promontory. Its diminutive is 'rosien', pronounced 'rushen', and was probably applied originally to Langness, the Isle of Man's only peninsula, and gradually came to mean the whole area.

The **fort** on **St Michael's Isle**, just off **Derbyhaven**, was probably built in the 1540s, and was named Derby Fort during the Civil War. It now houses a collection of cannon covering several centuries, and is owned by the **Manx National Trust**.

The constant overflying of planes to and from the adjacent **Ronaldsway Airport** is no excuse for not concentrating on your cricket … **King William's College** stands next to the Island's principal airport, whose growth in recent years is expected to continue to the point where within a decade a million passengers will pass through the terminal in the course of a year.

King William's also faces the sea, and a potent symbol for nationalists. **Hango Hill** is now just a tiny portion of a wall, but was in 1663 the place where it is believed the **Manx patriot**, **Illiam Dhone** (or 'William Christian'. The Manx version translates as 'Brown William') was executed by being shot. The site was originally a prehistoric burial mound, and was later used by the 7th Earl of Derby for a summerhouse. The remains of this house – most of which has now been washed into the sea – are still visible but it is possible the actual place of execution was nearer the College. This nicety has had no impact on the annual service of commemoration for Dhone's life which takes place on the 2nd January at Hango Hill each year.

The **lighthouse** at **Langness Peninsula**, built in 1880. The reefs and flat rocks around this coastline make it a particularly dangerous stretch to navigate.

Langness Peninsula with **St Michael's Isle** in the foreground. The **Castletown Golf Links Hotel** and the course dominates almost half of Langness itself. It might look as though the fairways don't go near the sea, but don't be deceived …

Across **St Michael's Island**, past **Derbyhaven** and **Castletown**, over **Bay ny Carrickey** to **Port St Mary**. Derbyhaven is where the first Derby race was run. The Earl of Derby was the Lord of Mann at the time, and in about 1645 he instigated a race with a prize worth about £5. There was a stipulation that only Manx horses could take part, reportedly because he felt they were the only ones capable of taking on the course. When his family returned to England, the race (and the name) went with them. It is now one of the world's great horse-racing occasions, held annually in Epsom, Surrey.

Many pictures in this book have caught sight of one of the major infrastructure works being undertaken by the Government of the Island, the IRIS project. But here in **Braddan** is another massive investment in the future of the Islanders – the new hospital. This is a figurehead for the Island's health services. At £111,730,000 it has not come cheap, but it provides over 300 beds, seven operating theatres and departments covering pharmacy to radiology. Designed by Davidson Marsh Barua - TAD, it is scheduled to open fully in spring 2003.

Left
A less romantic but nonetheless vivid panorama of **Douglas** shows the new business park, the large retail units, the spread of housing and (that patch of vivid green towards the top) the **National Sports Centre**.

Following pages
The business end. **Ballacottier Business Park** outside **Douglas** is the home of several HQs, including **Manx Telecom**.

The tree-line running diagonally across the picture is **Springfield** and **Farmhill Lane** in **Anagh Coar**.

Glen Vine, with the **Ballagarey** estate on the upper right is still under construction. Glen Vine has grown up over the last 30 to 40 years in **Marown**. Marown is the only parish on the Island not bordered at some point by the sea.

Manufactured landscape. The Island's hills and dales are now important as part of the attraction to visitors, and residents, rather than solely to be farmed or grazed. The **Mount Murray Golf Course** in **Santon** leaves its mark in the grass.

Below

Sitting on the outskirts of **Douglas**, the **National Sports Centre** represents a major investment in the sporting life of a hugely enthusiastic population. The buildings in the foreground contain the swimming pool and sports halls, while on the open-air part of the site there are all-weather pitches, and the arena for the field events is surrounded by the running track.

The newly completed **Douglas Head Apartments** dominate this view of Douglas Head. They were built around a stone watch-tower that was in place long before even the hotel that used to stand here. The fact that there are luxury flats rather than hotel rooms available at such a scenic spot is a significant indicator of the changes taking place in the Manx economy. Just above and to the right is the building that was the Headlands restaurant. The green box beyond that houses the old **Camera Obscura**, one of many entertainments that used to be found here in the busy tourism days. Opened in 1887, it has recently been rescued from complete destruction and awaits restoration. There has been a lighthouse in place since the 1830s, with the present one built in 1892. To the left of the apartment block is **Manx Radio**, the first commercial radio station in the British Isles, which started broadcasting (though not on this site) in 1964. The building was built during the Second World War to house trainee radar operatives, and as a result Douglas was the first commercial harbour to have the technology permanently installed.

The **lighthouse** and **Douglas breakwater**. The main building blocks of the breakwater are 'stabits'. These are two large concrete co-joined V shapes, which can interlock with each other with relative ease. 3,740 of them were used in the construction. They got their name from the motto on the Manx coat of arms. They were designed by a senior partner of the consultant engineers (Sir William Halcrow & Partners) who had been to Douglas High School. The Manx motto reads "Quocunque Jeceris Stabit" which roughly translates as 'Whichever way you throw it, it stands'. The word has made its way into the O.E.D., although that reference work does not include the Manx connection — yet.